Karen & Nathan Cobbs

Illustrated by Cheryl N. Hart, MA

Archway Publishing books may be ordered through booksellers or by contacting:

Archway Publishing
1663 Liberty Drive
Bloomington, IN 47403
www.archwaypublishing.com
1 (888) 242-5904

ISBN: 978-1-4808-5099-6 (sc)
ISBN: 978-1-4808-5100-9 (e)

Library of Congress Control Number: 2017950755

Print information available on the last page.

Archway Publishing rev. date: 11/29/2018

Dedicated to our very own Rosie Posie and Buddy.

You have overcome so much in your short life, Rosie. You are the most resilient, persistent, inquisitive, intelligent, sweet and funny little girl. Thank you for allowing us to share your story to help others.

Buddy, you have the biggest heart. You are the most loving, kind, smart, funny and supportive little boy. You complete our family and make it better in every single way.

We love both of you more than all the stars in the sky... all the fish in the ocean... and all ladybugs in the world. We are blessed and proud to be your parents.

Love,
Mommy & Daddy xoxo

Hi! My name is Rosie, but my friends call me Rosie Posie. I am a winter baby.

I was born during a blizzard and LOVE snow! Catching snowflakes with my younger brother, Buddy, is the best.

My family has fun making a snowman and snow angels.

I enjoy looking at Mr. Snowman outside my bedroom window.

Do you want to know something? Lean in closer, so our brains can talk. My words do not always come out of my mouth the way I want them to. I am still practicing!

Want to know something else? Ssshhhh! I will tell you something special about me.

I am like a real life super hero, because I have super senses. I am totally wonder-rific!

I have ALWAYS had a super sense of seeing, feeling, smelling, tasting, and hearing. Do you have super senses, too?

Some things still take me longer to learn than other kids my age, but that is okay. I will figure it all out, because I am super STRONG and really BRAVE!

My super sense of talking has not woken up yet, so my Mommy taught me a fun way to talk with my hands. It is called sign language.

This means I love you, because I Rosie-rific LOVE all my family and friends! Mommy adjusted the sign to make it very simple for me. I just make a big "X" across my chest. Will you try?

Sign language helps people understand me. That makes my super feelings HAPPY! Look, I will teach you a few signs.

This means drink...

This means eat...

I use the sign for "drink" when I am thirsty, because it's easiest for me. Make your hand into a "C" and pretend you are tipping a cup back and forth. When I am hungry, I use the sign for "eat" since it's simple, too. You just touch the tip of your thumb to your fingers. Move your hand back and forth gently tapping your mouth. People who don't know sign language even understand these signs, so I like them best!

I have a great sense of super seeing, but sometimes it is too good! The lights make my eyes and head hurt. Does the light ever hurt you?

Buddy brings me a teddy bear when I need a break from the light to rest my eyes. He is the BEST brother!

I love to wear hats and sunglasses in the bright sun. It really helps... and I look FAB-U-LOUS, too!

I have an extra good super sense of feeling. When I am nervous or overwhelmed, hugs really help me. Do hugs help you?

I also like when my Mommy squeezes the palm of my hand for a few seconds, then stops. She does this a few times in a row. Ahhhh, love it!

My kitty, Petey, cuddles in the tent with me when I need quiet time. My parents also got me a special weighted blanket. It feels SUPER Rosie-rific!

My super sense of feeling is amazing! Some days it is a little too amazing though. My clothes itch and hurt, so I take them off. We are late. A lot!

Mommy figured out if she dresses me in super soft clothes and underwear with no elastic or tags that it makes me HAPPY!! Aaaahhhh soooo much better!

My super senses go BONKERS when there is too much noise. Too many people in a small space is the WORST!

Often, I cry and run away even though I know this is unsafe. I need to STOP and use my super sign language instead!

Parties and new places are supposed to be fun... but they are usually too much for me. It helps when an adult tells me what to expect before we leave the house. We call this front loading.

We have a special super code for when I've had too much. It means "all-done" and that way we can go outside for a break, or go home.

This is the sign for "all-done" or "no more" and it is easy! You try. Just start with your palms facing your chest, and then turn your hands quickly so your palms are facing away from your chest. Sometimes I do it over and over if nobody notices the first time.

Do you want to know something else? I accidentally broke my finger on a table when I was younger. I could not stop moving and shaking my hands when I was very excited.

Since then, I try hard to clap or push my hands together like this instead. It feels Rosie-rific, not ouchy boo-boo!

Will you try it with me? Just put your hands together. Then, push in with both hands at the same time until you feel pressure. Hold it and count to ten in your mind before putting your hands down.

1... 2... 3... 4... 5... 6... 7... 8... 9... 10. Done. Way to go!

super
rosie
posie

Just like you, I am quite a fierce super hero. I have an extra good sense of super smell. Mmmmm flowers smell soooooo sweet! Buddy and Petey kitty even like them.

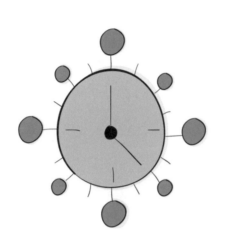

Garlic, onion, coffee and tacos stink though! PEE-YEW! I like to eat away from others. That makes them feel sad, but it makes me happy I do not have to smell the yuck.

Restaurants are the worst, because all the smells combine into one giant SUPER YUCK! Many times I run or cry, because it is too much for my nose.

My Mommy and Daddy want me to use my words and "done" super signal, so that I am safe. I am trying hard to remember!

Since we are friends, I will share this neat trick! If I eat the smelliest and spiciest food, then I can ONLY smell MY food. This way, I can eat with others. Sausage in a full moon circle is my favorite.

When I was little, my super taste powers were not wonder-rificly awesome. I refused to eat, because I could not taste my food. I got really weak and had to see doctors.

My parents tried this delicious orange spicy sauce on my food. Sometimes they add lemon juice or BBQ sauce on different food. It worked! My super taste buds woke up. Now I love to eat crunchy, salty, spicy and tart foods like green apples! Really hot or really cold food wake up my mouth and make me happy, too!

I especially love macaroni and cheese. The shell macaroni is my favorite, but it has to have a little crunch left in it. My Daddy makes the pasta really al dente. That is means crunchy in Italian!

But... I can't eat my mac without a few shakes of my favorite spicy sauce!

My super sense of hearing rocks! When I was a baby and my Daddy sneezed, I always cried. He sounded like a giant elephant... and scared me every time! AAAAAA-CHOO!!!

Super hearing can be fun, but sometimes one instrument sounds like a huge marching band. YOWZA!

I cover my ears when Buddy plays his horn or my family takes me noisy places. I want to run away with my super speed. Oh wait! I am working on the NOT doing that!

The wonder-rificly neat thing is that I can hear everything when others cannot. I am like a Rosie Posie detective!

When my super senses need a break, I just ask for some quiet time by making a giant letter "T" with my hands.

I do not even need to talk and can use this super sign. It means time out for peace and quiet. You try!

Many days we go on a nice, quiet walk together. Of course, I wear my super shades!

My family knows that I need super breaks often and that helps me feel Rosie-rific! I like to make cool patterns and designs with my toys.

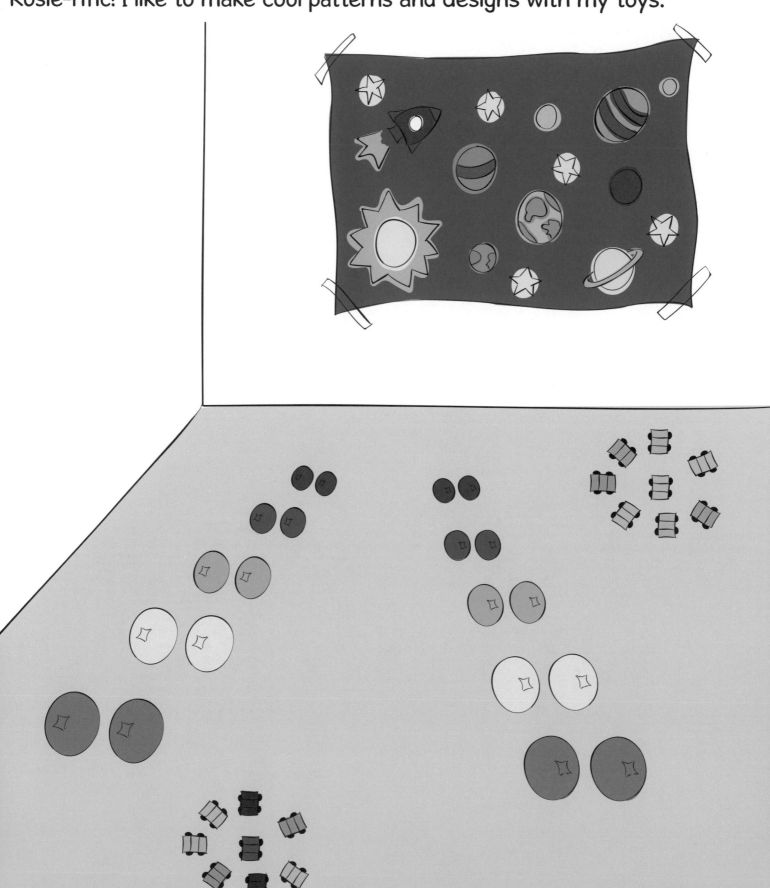

The stars, planets and maps are super interesting.
I love trains, cars, dinosaurs, puzzles and balls, too!

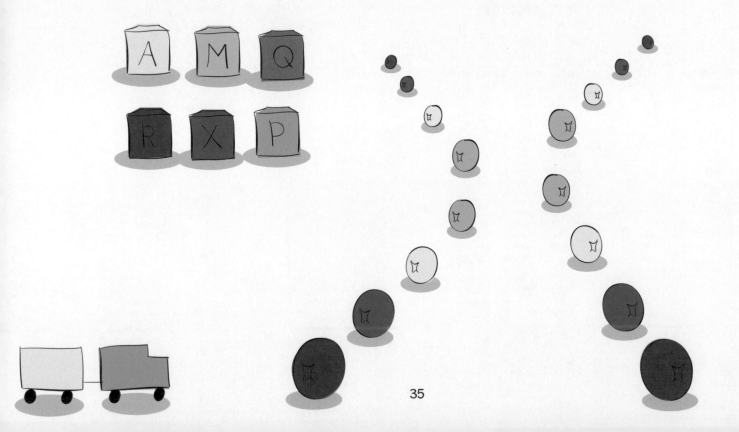

I am my own little super hero.
Unique, loved, and super smart!
I am my own special person. I
am wonder-rificly ME!

Just like you are wonder-rificly YOU!
I am so happy we are friends.

Printed in the United States
By Bookmasters